Raising Backyard Chickens

A Guide to Chicken Keeping

From Incubating Eggs, Caring for Chicks and Feeding Chickens to Egg Laying Hens and Fresh Eggs Daily

Introduction

Thank you so much for taking the time to purchase and download this book, *The Chicken Guide: Incubator to Egg Layer.*

So, you are thinking of raising chickens and have no clue where to start? Well, you have found just the book to help you from start to finish! This book covers what to expect when raising chickens, from egg to adulthood. In this book, you will find loads of helpful information to get the most out of your chicken raising experience.

Not just anyone has the ability to step into a chicken coop and be successful. But with this book, I assure you even the most inexperienced chicken folks will be able to raise and hatch their very own chicks with little to no issues! While it is a learning experience, this book will be the backbone to your cock-a-doodle-doo experience!

When I was contemplating getting chickens, other chicken owners would always warn me how addicting chicken keeping is and I now live the addiction! I started with five chickens about a year and a half ago and now we have 16 hens, 1 rooster, and 2 ducks. I have already ordered my spring chicks and ducks to add to the flock.

Once again, thanks for downloading this book, I hope you find it to be helpful and enjoyable!

Table of Contents

Chapter 1: Terms All Potential Chicken Owners Should Know

Chapter 2: Pros and Cons to Raising Your Own Chickens

Chapter 3: Pros and Cons to Hatching Your Own Chicks

Chapter 4: Choosing Eggs and Incubator Set-up

Chapter 5: Candling and the Growing Chick

Chapter 6: Hatching and Brooding

Chapter 7: Adolescence and Meeting the Flock

Chapter 8: Adulthood and Laying Eggs

Chapter 9: Things to Keep in Mind When Raising Your Own Chickens

Conclusion

Chapter 1: Terms All Potential Chicken Owners Should Know

To ensure you get the most information and value from the chapters that lie ahead of you, here is a list of the most used and popular chicken-related terms:

- **Bantam:** A chicken that is about ¼ of the size of a regular chicken, also referred to as a "miniature chicken."
- **Broiler:** A young chicken bred for meat. Broilers are typically butchered between 9 and 12 weeks of age and should weigh between 2.5 to 3.5 pounds. May also referred to as "fryers"
- **Brooder/brooder box**: An enclosure that is heated for the raising of chicks. Provides protection to chicks from drafts and predators as well as provides them access to water and food.
- **Brooding period:** The stage of a chick's life between when they hatch and they reach adulthood. Lasts from eight to ten weeks.
- **Broody hen:** A hen that sits on eggs to hatch and brood chicks.
- **Candling:** Process of shining a light on the egg to see the development of the embryo.
- **Chick starter:** Chicken feed that is high in protein and fed to chicks up to 8 weeks of age. May also be referred to as a starter feed.

- **Chick tooth:** The sharpest end of a chicken's beak that is utilized to poke a hole in the egg during the hatching process. Also referred to as "an egg tooth."

- **Cloaca:** The opening of a chicken in which the reproductive, urinary, and intestinal tracts empty.

- **Clutch:** A group of around 12 eggs. Commonly used when a group of eggs is being sat on or incubated by a broody hen.

- **Coccidiosis:** A disease fowl can catch that is caused by microscopic protozoa which attach to the intestinal lining. Causes diarrhea, weight loss, blood in stool, pale comb, and even death. Occurs more often in chicks that are less than 6 months old. This disease is transmitted by chicken feces and can be prevented with medicated chick starter feed or vaccinations.

- **Cock:** A male chicken that is over one year of age, referred to as "old rooster."

- **Cockerel:** A young male chicken that is less than one year old, referred to as "young rooster."

- **Comb:** The fleshy growth that is upon a chicken's head, which varies in shades of pink or red.

- **Culling:** Identifying and removing/butchering low egg producing or sick chickens from the flock.

- **Down:** The fine, soft feathers that are on baby chicks.

- **Dusting:** Also referred to as "a dust bath," it is a common chicken behavior where they bathe themselves with dust, dirt, or sand to rid themselves of parasites and mites.

- **Fount:** Watering device or a water fountain for chickens to drink from.

- **Gizzard:** An organ that is used to crush food with the assistance of grit or pebbles.

- **Grower feed:** A feed that is formulated for growing and adolescent chickens. Typically used from the 9 to 20-week mark.

- **Hen:** A female chicken that is over one year of age.

- **Incubator:** A container that artificially heats and simulates the environment needed for eggs to properly hatch.

- **Layers:** Matured female chickens that are kept for the production of eggs, also referred to as "laying hens."

- **Laying feed:** A feed that formulated for hens that are laying eggs. Given to chickens starting at 20 weeks of age.

- **Marek's disease:** A common viral disease that occurs in chickens. Prevented with a vaccination that is given to newly hatched chicks.

- **Molt:** The process an adult chicken goes through of losing and re-growing feathers. A hard molt is when a chicken loses and regrows many feathers whereas a soft molt is when a chicken loses and regrows few feathers.

- **Picking/Pecking:** A harmful activity among chickens where they peck at one another's feathers. This may be witnessed when chickens are establishing their pecking order.

- **Pipping:** The act of chicks who are pecking at their shells to break out during the hatching process.

- **Pullet:** A female chicken that is under one year of age.

- **Rooster:** A male, adult chicken.

- **Scratch:** A feed that is made from cracked corn and various kinds of whole grains. Fed as a treat to backyard chickens and not meant to be used as a main source of food.

- **Sexed chicks:** Chicks that have been separated by sex.

- **Straight-run chicks:** Chicks that have not yet been separated by sex.

- **Turn:** The turning of an incubated egg to prevent the embryo from sticking to the membranes of its shell.

- **Unthrifty:** A term used to describe chickens that are not healthy and are failing to thrive and/or fail to put on weight.

- **Wattles**: The red-colored and fleshy growths that hang off of the side of the beak or throat of a chicken.

Chapter 2: Pros and Cons to Raising Your Own Chickens

If you are considering raising your own backyard chickens, you need to be aware of the awesome advantages as well as the disadvantages that come along with this venture.

First things first, if you live within the limits of any city, you need to take the time to check with your city council to see if having and raising chickens is allowed in your city. If you raise chickens in a city that does not allow them, you can face a penalty. If you reside in a rural area, however, you should not have any issues with this.

Research and read about the pros and cons of raising your own chickens before attempting to grow a flock of your very own!

Pros to Raising Your Own Chickens

- **Fresh eggs**: If you are tired of paying the high prices for eggs, especially organic or cage free, having chickens lay fresh eggs right in your backyard can be a real bonus! Plus, if you have multiple hens, the more fresh eggs. I think they are much tastier than store-bought eggs. My eggs have a nice rich orangey yolk and firm shells compared to store-bought eggs.

- **Satisfying Meat**: Many people choose to raise chickens not necessarily for the eggs they produce, but for their meat. Store-bought chicken is becoming pricier each year, so why not raise your own meat! The best thing about this is that you know exactly what is in the chicken you gobble up. In my opinion, raising meat chickens is rewarding and humbling. I thought it would be difficult butchering our chickens but in the end, I know they had a happy and healthy life prior to providing food for my family.

- **Low-Maintenance**: While chickens do require a bit more than just feeding and watering, they are pretty simple to take care of compared to other animals and pets.

- **Cheap Upkeep**: The expense that you will incur on a day-to-day basis when raising chickens is minimal. For example, to raise and take care of three chickens, expect to spend around $25 per month on food and other miscellaneous expenses. The other nice thing about chickens is they will eat pretty much anything. Our chickens eat leftovers, table scraps, and produce and weeds from our garden.

- **A Lusher Lawn and Garden**: Chicken manure is an amazing natural fertilizer. If you are looking for ways to revive your garden and grass, having a few chickens around will surely do the trick. After harvesting your garden or starting a compost pile, let the chickens till up the dirt for you.

- **Pest Control**: Chickens love to explore and scratch around when they have the chance, which means that they will graze heavily on all those annoying weeds and bugs that are residing around your backyard. No need to treat your yard with chemicals since chickens love eating ticks and mosquitos!

- **An Unordinary and Fun Pet**: Chickens definitely have their own personalities and ours love attention. If you raise them from the time they are young and handle them often enough, you can easily hold and pet them. We currently have two buff Orpingtons and anytime they hear someone outside they come running from the barn to see what is going on. Also if they are out foraging in the yard and we head to the barn they come running to see what treats we are bringing for them.

Cons to Raising Your Own Chickens

- **Initial Costs Can Be Pricey**: Getting prepared to start your own flock from the ground up can be a bit pricey. You have to purchase hatching eggs or chicks/chickens, incubator if hatching, feed and water containers, feed, brooder, and a coop or shelter. The coop alone can cost an average of $500 if you do not build one yourself. We purchased our first coop from a farm supply store for around $300 and it was just large enough for five adult chickens.

- **Ordinances**: The rules of what is and is not allowed in the backyards of folks who live within city limits can vary from town to town. Make sure to check with your city regarding keeping farm animals on residential properties. The ordinances will sometimes limit the number of chickens allowed, ban roosters, or require the hens be caged at all times.

- **Potentially Unhappy Neighbors**: If you live in a town that allows you to raise chickens, you may find that you will have unhappy neighbors, despite your excitement about your new investment. Avoid buying a rooster or the noisier breeds of chickens and be generous with giving out your eggs to people who have to deal with the additional noise.

- **Incompatibility in Breeds**: Just like other animals, different breeds of chickens have their own traits. Some breeds are excellent egg-layers whereas others breeds tend to be more broody. Make sure to pick a breed that fits your lifestyle and climate. Otherwise, you might be left with troubles and headaches in the future.

- **Upkeep of the Coop**: While chickens are pretty low-maintenance, they are not zero-maintenance. To ensure the health of your chickens, you must make it a priority to keep the coop well ventilated, dry and clean, as well as supply a steady amount of food and water. If you travel a lot or despise the act of cleaning feces, you might want to reconsider your desire to own chickens. Chickens poop a lot!

- **Destructive Tendencies**: If you leave your chickens to roam around unsupervised, they can do some damage to your yard or garden because of their scratching. If you are one who loves your landscaped yard, chickens are probably not for you. We learned our lesson last summer and put up a fence around the garden to keep the chickens out.

- **Many Natural Predators**: Humans love chicken, but so do dogs, cats, coyotes, and other natural predators. Even if you take precautions, you will more than likely lose a few chickens through the ways of nature.

Chapter 3: Pros and Cons to Hatching Your Own Chicks

If you are considering going all into this chicken venture and taking it upon yourself to incubate your own eggs and successfully hatch them, it can be down-right rewarding and lead to many exciting possibilities. However, there are pros and cons that you need to consider.

Pros to Hatching Your Own Chicks

- **Ability to Add Variety to Your Current Flock**: Incubating eggs is an alternative to buying chicks to grow your flock. If you have a rooster, this can be a great opportunity to add mixed breeds and color variations to your flock.

- **A Rewarding and Fun Process:** While it is thrilling picking out chicks from a farm supply store, there is something about the excitement and anticipation of monitoring the progress of eggs whether using an incubator or a broody hen. The overall experience of hatching your own eggs is extremely fun and highly rewarding. Watching the eggs break open and reveal a fully formed chick is an experience all by itself!

- **Smoother Integration with the Flock:** A bonus of hatching your own eggs with a broody hen is she will care for the chicks and keep them warm. The hen will also protect the baby chicks from the flock.

Cons to Hatching Your Own Chicks

- **Cannot Select the Sex**: Many people avoid hatching their own eggs because around 50% of all eggs turn out to be males. For those who live in urban areas especially, this can be an issue when they have roosters causing noise issues. Re-homing roosters can be an issue as well. When you order chicks from a hatchery or buy pullets you can select the gender you want.

- **Cost:** The expense of hatching your own eggs is another factor you have to take into consideration. If you do not own a rooster, you will have to purchase fertilized eggs. Another thing to consider is if you purchase fertilized eggs they may be damaged during shipping. You may have to build or buy an incubator if you do not have a broody hen. I purchased a still air incubator from a farm supply store for about $35 dollars.

- **Time Commitment**: There is also the time management and dedication that is heavily involved in the successful hatching of baby chicks. Time and attention is a necessity for proper hatching. The fertilized eggs need to be turned three times a day and the temperature and humidity monitored closely. You can buy an incubator with an automatic egg turner but that will cost you around $100.

Chapter 4: Choosing Eggs and Incubator Set Up

Picking out the right eggs to incubate is important when you are starting the hatching process. If you desire a perfect hatch, you will need to begin by having the perfect eggs!

Factors that Influence the Hatchability of Eggs

- If the eggs were fertilized
- If the shell is in good shape
- The length of time the eggs were stored
- Time of the year

The Importance of the Time of Year

You strongly should consider the time of year in which you are choosing eggs to incubate. Chick incubation is recommended from February to March because they are able to forage during peak grass-growing season, which lasts usually from the end of March through June. After this batch, you should consider starting the next one in the late summer so that your chicks can take full advantage of the secondary peak of pasture from September to November.

If you are in the process of revitalizing your entire flock of chickens, it is crucial to have your chicks out of their shell by the middle of April at the latest. This ensures that they are old enough to lay eggs before fall begins. If you fail to do this, you risk feeding pullets that will not lay any eggs throughout the winter.

However, the biology of a chicken has the power to dictate a bit of a different pattern when it comes to hatching. Eggs are usually most fertile March through June, with a second peak of fertility in September and October. While you are not obligated to go by this, keep in mind that your results may not be as successful if you were attempting to raise chickens during the dead of winter.

Chick Parents

An issue that many come across when it comes to the overall health of the eggs they choose lies within the parents that created them. If you are familiar with chicken breeding and raising, you have probably heard that you are supposed to keep the flock that is responsible for breeding in green pastures, since they are full of nutrition that results in highly hatch-able eggs.

While this might be true, there are many others who found that when the breeding flock consumes more bugs than greenery, have brighter egg yolks and higher hatch rates.

What you feed your breeders is not the only crucial factor in producing hatch-able eggs. Roosters and hens that are newly sexually active or are more than two years of age tend to create fewer eggs that have a good fertility rate. Even though your hens are still laying eggs, this does not mean that the egg embryos are viable enough to mature.

Roosters, of course, are a pertinent piece of the puzzle when it comes to fertilizing eggs. There have been people who struggle with their rooster not mating enough to produce fertilized eggs. To combat this, keep fewer hens than the suggested dozen per rooster. This will ensure that your rooster does not have too much hard work ahead of him.

Inbreeding

Inbreeding is a common issue for backyard chicken raisers. You will need to trade roosters with others probably every year, or purchase an entirely new round of straight run chickens to raise a brand-new rooster on an annual basis. This will help to ensure that the hens are not mating with fathers and brothers. Inbreeding greatly decreases the hatch rates and can lead to the production of sick chicks from the eggs that do manage to hatch.

Picking Great Eggs Step-By-Step

Choosing eggs from your very own flock leads to few issues, since you know your hens and how they are cared for. However, if you are just starting out, you will be choosing eggs from the production of someone else's hard work, which can be challenging. Here are some good pointers and steps to follow when picking eggs that will have a high hatch rate.

Step One: Check the source

If you are picking eggs that are not from your own flock, ensure that you purchase them from a reliable source. If you are buying from places like Craigslist or eBay, these sources are not always dependable, and sellers could honestly be selling anything to you. Opt to go to a local, independent breeder to give yourself peace of mind.

If at all possible, ask to see the flock that you are buying from for yourself. If you get this chance, keep an eye out for free-range and highly active hens who are dwelling in a healthy environment and are fed a good diet. These ladies will be the ones that lay well-formed, clean, and strong eggs that have the optimum chance of hatching.

You can also purchase fertilized eggs from well-known, reputable hatcheries online who ship the eggs directly to you. While this is riskier, just ensure that the seller is packaging them with the label "fragile." If they are to be sent to a post office, contact the staff to let them know that you are expecting them and to have them call you as soon as they come in. Make sure to collect them as soon as you can.

Eggs that have traveled need to be allowed to rest twelve hours at the minimum before they are placed in any kind of incubator. Remove them from the packaging and store them with the smaller end facing down. When you are storing hatching eggs, make sure you keep them in an area that is cool but not too cold, and that is moist. You can store the eggs at room temperature down to 60 degrees.

Step Two: Check the Age

So, how old can an egg be to still hatch successfully? Eggs should be placed in an incubator 7-10 days after being laid. The process of fertility starts to fall after this timeframe, which will result in lower hatch rates.

If you hatch eggs that are older than this, however, the hatch rate will not be nearly as high, but some could hatch if stored properly.

Step Three: Check the Eggs

If you are receiving eggs via the post office, you may experience a high volume of eggs that have a detached air cell, which is caused by being jolting around during delivery. These eggs have a very poor hatch rate. You will be able to see a "saddle shape" form after a few days of candling in an incubator if an air cell has detached itself.

When you are choosing eggs from a group, pick out ones that are normal in their shape. If they look long, are rounded at both ends, or are pitted, put that one back and choose ones that are in optimal shape. Remember to select eggs that look typical and characteristic for the breed of chicken.

Do not select eggs that have any cracks no matter how tiny. These eggs have a very low hatch rate since a crack can lead to dangerous contamination of other eggs in an incubator. Do not rely on your plain eyesight to spot cracks, because you will miss hairline fractures in the shell. Instead, use a candling device or a bright light to see under the egg.

Is the egg you have chosen a bit porous in nature? Some people throw these out, but there are many others who have still had success with porous eggs. Under a candling light, a porous egg will look rather mottled. A slight indication of mottling is not unusual, but the more porous it is, the less likely it is to hatch.

Step Four: Following Simple Rules for Hatching Success

Make sure when you are choosing hatching eggs that they are as clean as they can be. Putting extremely dirty eggs into an incubator can cause bacteria, which can be fatal to growing embryos. There are different options to clean eggs, depending on just how much dirt is on them. You can simply scrape the dirt off with your fingernail. But if this is not enough, you can use sandpaper to gently scrape it as well. Just be very careful not to crack the egg or rub dirt into the pores of the shell.

If the egg still looks too dirty to incubate, there is also the option of cleaning it with water. Use tepid, not cold water. There is also a washing disinfectant that is specifically made for eggs, but some people just use a diluted bleach solution. Many people do not like bleach solutions and just clean their eggs for incubation in warm water. If you wash the dirty eggs make sure to wash all eggs since eggs that appear clean may still have bacteria on them.

After you have completed all of these steps successfully, you are now ready to incubate your eggs!

Everything You Need to Know About Incubation

Mothering chicken eggs is not everyone's forte, but if you want to try it out or cross it off of your bucket list, then the following section is vital to your success!

When a hen lays eggs, mothering instincts take hold. They fuss over them, adjust them throughout the day and rarely if ever, leave the nest for more than just a few minutes. Motherhood for any creature is a giant responsibility, especially for young hens. If they are even a bit too neglectful, there is a big chance that the eggs they laid will not hatch, or if it does hatch, will do so with deformities.

There are certain chicken breeds that make better mother hens compared to others. Some chicken breeds are bred in an attempt to make them less likely to go broody. Other factors that could affect the hen's willingness to continue sitting is other mother hens taking over the nest or if the hen and her eggs are moved.

Some backyard farmers do not trust the incubation process of hens, so they take it upon themselves to put in the work. There is also the option to buy chicks that are a day old and skip over the entire incubation process, but this can be rather pricey in the long run. Why miss out on the opportunity to see one of life's greatest miracles?

Step One: Setting Up your Incubator

The type of incubator you choose to buy depends on just how many eggs you plan to hatch at a time. There are incubators as cheap as $40 while others run into the thousands of dollars. Commercial grade incubators are as simple as putting in the eggs, closing the door and not doing anything for three weeks.

The do-it-yourself process takes more work but is a lot less money. If you go this route, be prepared for a lot of work to ensure that your chicks hatch. No matter how basic or fancy, all incubators must perform these basic things for the hatchlings to survive and thrive:

- **Temperature** of eggs should be kept at 99.5 degrees all the time. Even just one degree higher or lower for as little as a couple hours can terminate the embryo.
- The **humidity** must be maintained between 40-50 percent for the first 18 days, then 65-75 percent for the final days before hatching.

- The shells of eggs are porous in nature, so **ventilation** is vital to allow oxygen to enter and carbon dioxide to exit the egg. Incubators have proper holes and vents to let fresh air in so the fetuses can adequately breathe.

DIY Incubator

Do it yourself versions of incubators typically are made from:

- An **insulated box**, even a Styrofoam cooler would do the trick.

- A **light bulb** or an adjustable heating pad to create a heat source.

- A **pan of water paired with a sponge** to create the humidity eggs need.

Low-end incubators that you can purchase do not amount to much more than what you can make yourself, however, the more you pay, the more automatic the humidity and temperature controls will be.

Must-Have's for Incubators

Whether you make a DIY incubator or splurge on a high-end one, you will need both a high-quality **hygrometer**, a tool to measure the humidity and a high-quality **thermometer** to monitor temperature. These are vital to incubation, and you should not go cheap when purchasing these items. Some incubators are equipped with an LED sensor that shows the temperature and humidity without having to open and close the incubator, which could ruin a calibrated environment.

One of the best things about a fancier, more expensive incubator is the time-saving feature of rotating the eggs automatically. When mother hens fuss over their eggs, they are essentially rotating them and moving them around. This fine tunes the environment within the egg to adjust the position of the embryo. High-end devices have this built in, but egg turners can be placed in a homemade incubator as well or you can opt to rotate them by hand.

Based on my personal experience with a still air incubator that required us to hand turn eggs, I have decided I will purchase an egg turner. I also did not buy an expensive hydrometer, which I think caused our hatch to be unsuccessful. I thought it was difficult to maintain the temperature and humidity in our incubator, which I have read is more difficult to do in a still air incubator compared to circulating air incubators.

You should place your incubator in a location where the temperature does not fluctuate much. A basement is the best option, while by a window should be avoided.

Step Two: Incubate

On average, it takes 21 days for an egg to successfully hatch once the incubation process is started. Before you place any eggs into an incubator, turn on your source of heat and accurately measure the humidity and temperature for 24-hours. Make adjustments as you see fit to help in the creation of an optimal environment for your eggs.

If the humidity is too low or high, use a bigger or smaller sponge. Lower and raise the temperature of the heat source in small increments until the thermometer reads 99.5.

Once you have maintained the temperature and humidity, it is time to put the eggs in! Make sure you shut the door to your incubator all the way and make it a priority to regularly check the temperature and humidity levels. You may need to add water to the pan on occasion to keep the humidity at a proper level. When you hit day 18 of the incubation process, place more water into the pain to boost overall humidity.

If you plan to turn the eggs by hand, there is a specific method you should use to mimic the actions of a mother hen:

- Draw an 'X' on one side and an 'O' on the other side of each egg with a pencil. This helps you keep track of which eggs have been turned.

- Gently turn over the eggs at least three times a day. The more frequently you turn them, the better, but make sure to make the number of times you turn them is an odd number. This ensures that the eggs are not resting on the same side two nights in a row.

- Continue this method of turning until you reach day 18. At this point, you need to leave the eggs alone for the remaining incubation time as tempting as it can be.

Chapter 5: Candling and the Growing Chick

It is a good idea and a great practice to keep track of how the eggs are coming along in their development by candling the eggs.

Candling is a process that involves shining a bright light into the egg so that you can see the egg's contents and check to see if it is properly developing. It is important to remember that you may not have a 100 percent hatch rate. You will get some eggs that are not fertile from the get-go, known as yolkers, and others that will stop developing at some point during the process of incubation, known as quitters.

Candling gives you the ability to identify which eggs are quitters and yolkers. This will prevent them from bursting or rotting in your incubator, contaminating the healthy and properly developing eggs with a very bad smell and harmful bacteria.

Candling Equipment

To perform candling, there is no need to spend a lot of money on fancy equipment. Back in the good old days, candling used to be done simply using a candle, which is where the name of the process came from!

The main requirement for candling properly is a very bright light source so that you can view the inside of the egg better. You will need to head to a dark room to be able to see inside the egg. You can get a candling light from a poultry or farm supply store, which is essentially a small flashlight powered by a cord or batteries. I purchased my candling light for around $7.

You can make your very own candling device that works just as efficiently by using a 60-watt light build inside of a coffee can. Create a hole that is an inch in diameter in the top of the can. You could also take a bright flashlight and cover the opening with a piece of cardboard with a hole in the center.

Stick to a Candling Schedule

You should take the time to properly candle your eggs before adding them to your incubator. You more than likely will not see much, but it can help determine the difference between good and bad eggs, and give you a good indication as to what an undeveloped egg looks like in comparison to a healthy one.

Look for any tiny cracks that are not visible to the naked eye. Cracked eggs can be susceptible to bacteria that could get inside the shell and harm the embryo. Do not discard cracked eggs right away, but be sure to jot down the crack as you continuously check the egg's progress.

Some people candle their eggs daily during incubation, however, it is recommended to start candling after a week. The reasons behind this suggestion are:

- Eggs are very sensitive to temperature. Moving them in and out of the incubator could affect their overall development, especially during the earliest stages.

- Eggs will not have developed very much before day seven, so it will be rather challenging to know the difference between good and bad eggs.

After candling on day seven, leave the eggs alone until day fourteen. You will be able to check the eggs you are uncertain about during this time and discard them if there are no signs of development.

Do not candle after day eighteen because the eggs should not be moved or turned during this time since these are the crucial days leading up to hatch day. The embryos will be almost fully developed by this point and fill the egg, so you will be able to see very little.

How to Candle Your Eggs

Set up your candling equipment in a dark room that is close to your incubator. Pick out any egg from your incubator and hold it above the light. Here are the correct steps to properly and carefully candle:

1. Position the larger end of the egg against the light. This is where the air sac is located. Hold the egg close to the top, between your forefinger and thumb. Tilt it a bit to one side and rotate it until you get a good view.

2. Mark each egg with a number and take notes to keep track of your observations. This will help you to compare results from the first candling to the second.

3. Work fast, but not so quickly that you drop your eggs. Make sure you return your eggs to the incubator within 20-30 minutes of removing them for candling, so you do not affect their development. This will imitate a mother hen, who leaves her eggs for short periods of time during the incubation period.

4. It is more challenging to candle speckled or brown eggs that have dark shells since they are not as transparent with a light source.

Signs of Good Eggs

Winner eggs are the ones you strive for! They are the ones that have a successfully developing embryo within them. Here is how you can tell if you have a winner egg while you candle:

- You should be able to see a network of blood vessels that spread from the center to the outward edges of the egg.

- When using a weaker source of light, you should be able to decipher a clear bottom half and a darker top half. The bottom is where the air sac is, while the top half is where the embryo is developing.

- With a good source of light, you should be able to see an outline of the embryo located in the center of the network of vessels. You should be able to see the embryo's eyes, which look like dark spots inside the egg.

- If you are lucky, you may catch the embryo moving!

Signs of Bad Eggs

Also known as "quitters," bad eggs are determined by the cease of development at some point during the incubation process. Some simply stop developing because of a lack of maintained temperatures, while others may have been contaminated by bacteria, or some just because they were made with poor genes. Here are the signs of a bad egg:

- Blood rings are a definite indicator of a bad egg. A blood ring will appear as a circle that is well-defined and red, visible on the inside of the shell. This is created when the embryo dies and the vessels that were supporting it detach from the embryo and float in the yolk.

- Bad eggs may also have blood spots or streaks inside the shell. Be aware that the dark patches can be difficult to distinguish from a healthy egg, especially during the early stages.

- If you are certain that the egg is a quitter, you should throw it out right away to prevent it from going bad, exploding within your incubator and contaminating other good eggs.

Signs of Yolker Eggs

Yolker eggs are ones that failed to be fertilized and have no chance of ever creating an embryo. Here are the signs to determine if an egg is a yolker:

- The inside of the egg is clear, with no appearance of blood rings, blood vessels, or dark spots.

- The egg appears to be the same as the first time you candled the eggs.

If you are unsure as to what your egg identifies as do not trash it. Just make a note on these eggs by gently marking them with a question mark and put them back into the incubator. It is always worth a shot! Go back and check those questionable eggs again on day fourteen. If there are still no signs of development or if you see a blood ring, you can then discard them.

Chapter 6: Hatching and Brooding

If you have followed the previous chapters closely, congratulations! You are now ready to see the magic of baby chicks hatching and coming into this world!

The First 24 Hours After Hatching

You probably watched in awe as all your hard worked paid off seeing the incubated eggs turn into fluffy little hatchlings. Now that the chicks are out of their shells, what do you do?

Do not fret too much over the little chicks. Hatching is an "eggs-hausting" process, and the chicks are in need of some well-deserved rest after hatching. If you see that they are panting or slumped over, you might panic, but they are just tired from the entire hatching business.

You may also notice that the newly hatched chicks appear damp, which may tempt you to dry them off. No worries, they will fluff up on their very own in a few hours. It is vital to not move the chicks from the incubator or mother hen until they have had a chance to fluff up and dry off. Otherwise, they may get sick from catching a chill.

Once the chicks hatch, they will instinctively go to the membrane and yolk of the egg and gobble it up, for it has loads of nutrients for them. Because of this, you will not need to worry about feeding them until 1-2 days after they hatch since they fill themselves up on the nutrients from their shell.

After the first couple days, you must keep feed and water readily available to the chicks once they are dismissed from the incubator. Never let feed or water run out!

It has been suggested by many chicken-raising experts to actually incorporate a type of vitamin water the first day or so and then add feed later on. They have also suggested preparing a boiled egg for them to eat, for it is a great protein source for the rapidly growing chicks. Mash up a bit of chicken feed with the boiled egg along with some plain yogurt. This mixture helps the natural flora in their guts to kick-start. Supplying baby chicks with good nutrition is vital to the growing of a good flock.

In the first 24 hours, however, it is pertinent that you encourage the chicks to consume some water. If the chicks are hatched naturally from a mother hen, she is responsible for teaching them about drinking water. But if you raised them in an incubator, you are responsible for teaching them to drink! Place a baby chicken water feeder within the incubator. You will need to gently dip their beak into the water to encourage them to drink. Make sure to only put a baby chick sized water source in their incubator, otherwise they might drown. This means you need to have patience and persistence until the chicks drink on their own.

Another important task when your chicks first hatch is to properly and consistently clean their bedding. You will probably need to change it multiple times per day since it is crucial to their health that it is clean. Do not use newspaper as bedding, since it can become slippery and cause splayed legs in chicks.

Whatever you do, **do not** take the eggs not yet hatched out of the incubator. Do not assume that just because some have hatched, the rest will. You never know when an egg is going to hatch precisely. It is vital to keep the unhatched eggs in the incubator for another 24-48 hours after the first ones begin to hatch. In fact, the chirping of the hatched baby chicks will help to encourage others to come out of their shell. Even when you take the hatched chicks out of the incubator, leave the other eggs in there for another 24 hours, just to be safe.

When It Comes Time to Brood Your Chicks

Once your chicks have hatched, the next step is moving them out of the incubator and into the brooder. Brooding is the period after hatching to the time no supplemental heat is needed for their survival. For most chicken keepers, this means that the new chicks need to be kept indoors under a heat lamp for three to eight weeks. The smaller and slower the breed naturally is, the longer the brooding process will be.

The brooding process is a very crucial time in a baby chick's development. They are creatures that grow rapidly and are unable to handle outdoor environments since they are not capable of regulating temperature like adult chickens can. This makes them susceptible to diseases.

There are six essential pieces to the brooding process that all chicken keepers have to remember:

1. Lighting and Temperature
2. Ventilation and Humidity
3. Bedding
4. Feed
5. Water
6. Mortality

Lighting and Temperature

The lighting you choose fills two basic needs: warmth and light to see. The majority of backyard chickens are raised with heat lamps hung over the brooder. These lights are easy to find at farm supply stores or online and are inexpensive. The temperature created by a warming light is adjusted by raising and lowering the light fixture. Remember to never hang lights by their electrical cord, as this is a way to encourage a fire to occur. Instead, utilize a chain or rope.

While it sounds simple to adjust the temperature of your brooder by changing the position of the light, it can be troublesome. You should keep a thermometer in the brooder and a thermometer on the edge as well, with at most a 10-degree distinction between the two thermometers. Diverse chick ages have specific temperature requirements; on the first day keeping the temperature at 90 to 95 degrees and reduce by 5 degrees each week.

Generally, people follow the cluster rule: If your chicks are grouped all under the light, it is too cold for them, and if your chicks are crowded around the edge of the brooder, it is too warm for them. Ideally, they ought to be spread all through the brooder to easily move around.

One thing to keep in mind as you maintain the temperature of your brooder by techniques other than warming lights, is that chickens are typically not great at self-preservation. Utilizing a heating pad can cause burning on their feet, and utilizing a standing radiator can burn the chicks or overheat them as the ones behind push towards the heat source. Overhead heat sources, such as pan brooders, are the safest heating in order provide your chicks with the perfect temperature to remain comfortable and safe in the brooder.

Ventilation and Humidity

Just like light and warming, ventilation and humidity are related. High ventilation lowers humidity by blowing the water vapor in the air all around, while low ventilation can make mugginess too high. Adjusting the ventilation and humidity tends to be simple in brooding circumstances, however, the balance is more troublesome the bigger the size of the flock.

Ventilation is essential for the prevention of ammonia fumes; any individual who has brought up chicks in an enclosed area knows how powerful the scent in an unclean brooder can become. Nonetheless, you should be mindful so you do not end up with too much ventilation creating drafts that cool the chicks too much. Most brooders with an open top or a mesh/wire top will provide satisfactory ventilation. High-sided tubs or enclosed barns might not have satisfactory ventilation near the floor where the chicks dwell, regardless if the air flows through higher in the structure.

Humidity is not as much an issue in the prevention of ammonia fumes. Few small brooders are completely enclosed allowing high levels of humidity. Check your bedding to ensure it is not damp; if the bedding is dry the humidity should be fine. In the event that the litter is damp and you do not believe the chicks will get chilled, you can create ventilation as an attempt to dry the litter. You can purchase a hygrometer to measure the humidity in the brooder but typically natural humidity is fine.

Bedding

There are two fundamental guidelines for brooder bedding:

- Change it regularly
- Change it well

In smaller flocks, changing your bedding is the ideal approach to prevent the development of diseases, smell, and mold. Utilizing a litter that is absorbent in nature is vital: Pine shavings and rice hulls are ideal. Straw, hardwood shavings (especially oak) and paper are not great alternatives even though they are popularly used. Straw does not soak up water from feces very well and tends to promote the formation of mats. Proper bedding will provide absorption and reduce the smell and dust, which will diminish infection and mortality.

Feed

At what point do you encourage a starter versus a layer versus a grower diet? And what is the difference between all of these types of feed anyway?

Starter feed, also called chick starter, is formulated for your rapidly growing chicks and can be used as a starter for meat and layer breeds. It is high in protein—around 20 percent—and should be consumed for the first eight weeks of life.

The length of time you should feed your chickens a certain feed depends on the breed. Moderate developing show breeds require nutritional support for longer periods, while quickly developing birds, such as meat birds, are ready for a grower feed within a couple weeks. Layer and show breeds switch to a layer feed around 18-20 weeks. Since meat birds develop quicker, they are changed to a finisher feed a few weeks prior to butchering.

Feed is regularly sold as medicated, which implies it contains a medicine called amprolium, which is utilized only for the treatment of coccidiosis. Coccidiosis is caused by living beings called protozoa that live in the chickens' digestive tract. Fortunately, amprolium is an antiparasitic: which means it kills off these protozoa by denying them thiamine, a fundamental supplement. If you vaccinate your chickens then you would not want to feed them medicated feed. Fortunately, there has been an increase of natural and drug-free feed choices over the last 10 years. Most supply stores that sell feed offer alternative choices to the primary brands.

You need to consider how feed is dispensed to your flock. Chicks in their initial days of life require available nourishment. Place paper down under the heat lights with feed sprinkled on it for the initial couple of days, with food in a semi-open to open compartment at the edge of the brooder away from the light.

Trough feeders are the best, as most have a rooftop connection with head holes for when the chicks are older to keep them from defecating in the feeder. Bell feeders are another great choice for older chicks as well; simply be watchful with smaller chicks, as they may attempt to move inside the feeder and become stuck.

Water

A good rule of thumb is to use the type of waterer that the chicks will use as adults. If your flock drinks from a container or bell drinker as a grown-up, you ought to have a bell waterer for them as chicks. If you are lucky enough to get nipple drinkers within your group, chicks should be started by drinking water from this system. Do not use an open dish or container with water in a brooder, as chicks can fall in and drown or become chilled.

You should change the water twice per day to lessen fecal, feed or bedding from contaminating the water. Water systems should be cleaned or flushed with vinegar on a weekly basis to prevent the development of bacteria or mold. Waterers should be easily accessible.

Mortality

As discouraging as it is, mortality is a reality with brooding. Regardless of how perfect your framework, there will inevitably be deaths. Some of these might be from poor chick quality, pecking or starvation from rivalry. A small amount of mortality is possible however high amounts of mortality is an indicator that something is going wrong. Make sure to keep close track of your losses so you know what might be going wrong so that you can quickly figure out what the cause of excess mortality may be.

Expect to lose 1 to 2 percent of your chicks during the first time of brooding. This number can increase if they become infected, obtained from a poor breeding stock, become dehydrated, or chilled. Losing more than this amid your first week is a good indicator that you should choose another source to obtain hatching eggs. Monitor your misfortunes and assess your incubating and brooder set up, your underlying management habits, and your management of long-term brooding.

In the event that you do begin having exorbitant mortality, a necropsy is something to consider. Necropsies can help you to depict the reasoning for deaths, which can help with prevention of this issue in the future. Contact your state research facility for necropsy services; a few states sponsor this administration.

Chapter 7: Adolescence and Meeting the Flock

You will quickly realize that your chicks are growing quickly and most likely outgrowing their brooder space. The next step is integrating your new birds with the rest of the flock. This can be a stressful time for both you and your chickens. During the introduction of your new chicks to the existing flock, you will witness the "pecking order." The older chickens will make sure the chicks know their place at the bottom. Stressed chickens are more likely to become ill.

Nutrition

While much consideration is given to chick nutrition, this may be put to the wayside once you integrate them with the flock. It may seem convenient to give everyone a layer feed but remember to keep the young chickens on chick starter until they are around 18-20 weeks old or begin to lay eggs. Once you mix them with the older hens it is hard to keep their feed separate so I usually mix half chick starter and half layer feed.

The nutrition of your adolescent chickens affects how well the chicken's reproductive systems will develop. Utilizing the right eating routine is fundamental to prevent laying-related troubles and illnesses during the hen's adulthood. Changing to a laying feed before the bird has reached four months of age can be harmful.

Each flock owner can decide when their birds are coming nearer to the age of laying by the pullet's comb. Combs change from thin, pale, and dry to a more waxy, full, and red condition as the pullet nears laying age. Once you start to notice these changes in your pullets, you can begin adding layer feed to the diet gradually.

Development of the Immune System

In spite of the fact that the immune system of all birds will continually change and adjust throughout their life, the first couple of months are the most essential to the future protection against diseases. A proper introduction to the flock enables your younger chickens to be acquainted with any potential air-borne sicknesses gradually so they can create immunities without being overpowered by potential ailments. An overpowered immune system is not healthy and could be harmful to your chickens. Enable the younger chicks to battle, overcome, and shield themselves from adult ailments.

Instead of integrating pullets and cockerels into the flock right away from the raising pens, they should be introduced slowly. For instance, at around two months or when they are fully feathered, the young chickens can be placed in the same area as the rest of the flock while not being with the flock itself. One way to do this is have a wire cage/kennel or an enclosed fenced area in the barn or coop. This way the young chickens are protected from bullying and pecking from the older chickens but can see and hear each other. I would keep the young chickens separate for at least a week so everyone can get used to each other.

The first time you allow the chickens to mingle, it is a good idea to observe the flock's behavior for the first couple of days. A little pecking is completely normal as the flock re-establishes the pecking order so do not be alarmed. I have noticed that some of my chickens tend to be a little dramatic and make a lot of noise for a little peck here and there.

Chapter 8: Adulthood and Laying Eggs

At four to five months of age, all that care and nourishment begins paying off in delicious fried eggs and omelets– your chickens are all grown up and laying their first eggs! Beginning around 20 weeks of age, the time has come to change your flock to a total layer feed. Layer feeds usually contain 16% protein and expanded levels of calcium, a key supplement for solid and strong eggshells.

Picking a layer feed made with high-quality ingredients is important since whatever your hens are consuming passes through to the eggs they create. This is the reason there are many chicken feeds and supplements defined with Omega-3, like Manna Pro Omega Egg Maker, which can be blended in with your flock's total layer feed. Some chicken keepers use organic feed, which contains non-GMO ingredients that are grown without the utilization of engineered composts or pesticides.

At this age, you may give chicken treats or scratch grains to help keep your birds engaged. Remember treats are to be given in moderation and the primary source of food should be a layer feed. Do not give more than the chickens can eat in 15-20 minutes. Poultry grit should be provided to assist with appropriate digestion, which are tiny pebbles that you can buy at farm supply store. If you are able to let your chickens free range and wander around the yard, they will pick for small stones in the dirt or sand.

Make sure to keep the nesting boxes clean since most hens do not like laying eggs in a messy box. Your eggs will be cleaner as well. Attempt to gather eggs twice every day at minimum once per day. This will prevent eggs from sitting out too long or getting dirty and will keep chickens from pecking the eggs. I put golf balls in my nesting boxes to encourage the new layers to lay in the designated spot.

Many factors influence the number of eggs your hen will lay each week. The breed plays a major role in egg production since some breeds, like leghorns, are better known as prolific layers. Poor nourishment and extreme fluctuations in temperature could decrease egg production. Lighting has a tremendous effect since chickens need about 14-16 hours of daylight to produce the hormone to produce an egg.

The health of chickens is another a factor in the production of eggs. Vermin, lice, and mites are avoidable pests and parasites. Giving your flock a container full of sand or dirt so they can give themselves dust baths is the first step to preventing parasites. Another thing to add into the dust bath is wood ash. We have a pellet stove and throw cooled ash from our stove in the barn. Wood ash is a natural remedy and preventative for parasites. Respiratory sicknesses are best counteracted through proper coop ventilation and good sanitation practices. Always be sure to separate any chickens that appear ill to prevent the spread of disease within the flock.

In the event that a hen is pecked to the point of bleeding, it is essential to stop this abuse from occurring. Unfortunately, a forceful hen can truly peck another chicken to death! Adequate space, roosting areas, and food sources help prevent pecking, as well as toys and treats that bust boredom. Consider hanging a cabbage or provide a pecking block for the hens to peck at rather than each other. Unbreakable mirrors or other reflective objects will be sure to entertain as well. Your chickens will also love to explore the yard or chicken run if given the opportunity.

Chapter 9: Things to Keep in Mind When Raising Your Own Chickens

This chapter is dedicated to loads of valuable information for your first steps among a life with chickens.

Build a coop or purchase one already made

Chickens do not care how fancy the coop is as long as it is functional and provides adequate space. You could build a coop using recycled and scrap material you have laying around the yard or garage. If you do not think you can build your own chicken coop, there are many options to purchase from farm supply stores or online.

Pick/build the right chicken coop

Make sure your coop provides adequate space for the size of your flock. The rule of thumb is about 3 square feet per chicken. Another good option is to have a run for your chickens to graze and to get some fresh air. Remember the coop needs to have nesting boxes for a place to lay eggs and a roosting bar or area with plenty of room for sleeping. I suggest having one nesting box for every 3-4 hens.

Find chicken farmers near you

While you can find a ton of information about raising backyard chickens in books and online, no information is as valuable as the knowledge that comes straight from a seasoned chicken keeper! Seeing other people's setups will help you in creating your own.

Grazing

If you do not have a fenced backyard, simply purchase a pen in which your chickens can graze in. The average dog pen works perfectly fine. Just ensure that the wall of the pen you get is high enough so your chickens will not fly out. It is not a bad idea to put wire or netting across the top of the pen to prevent eagles or hawks from swooping in.

Be prepared for chicken deaths

This is yet another good reason to create a sturdy coop for your chickens to stay safe in. From neighborhood dogs and cats to raccoons, weasels, and other natural predators, you will and should prepare yourself to witness the aftermath of gruesome deaths. I use cloth wire around the run and barn, which we have buried 12 inches out from the fence and up the bottom of the fence about two feet. Some chicken wire has holes big enough for your chickens to stick their heads through which makes them vulnerable to predators.

It is possible you will have a rooster in the brood

Sexing chicks is not 100% accurate so you may end up with a rooster or two. It may be against the rules to have a rooster in urban and suburban areas. The crowing may annoy some people, especially your neighbors. So be prepared to find him a new home, or you might have to eat him for dinner.

Don't expect eggs on a consistent schedule

While the breed of chicken helps you determine when chickens begin to lay eggs, they may take longer than the estimated time. Egg laying will also vary with the seasons. Make sure that your hens have quality feed with protein and adequate amounts of water to encourage consistent egg laying.

Spend time on blogs

Just like human or pet parents, indulge in information found on the internet via blogs to gather valuable information to ensure the health and well-being of your flock. This is also a great way to read Q&A to learn about other's personal experiences raising chickens. You will be surprised how many are out there! Here are a few to check out:

- The Chicken Chick
- Backyard Poultry Magazine
- Backyard Chickens.com
- My Pet Chicken

Farm life is not all roses

While there are materials that help to keep the odor down, chickens still produce lots of waste, which attract flies and can be gross to be around. The best thing to do is clean and replace the soiled straw or bedding on a weekly basis or as often as needed.

Chicken Entertainment

You will come to enjoy watching the behavior and interactions among your chicken flock. They will have different personalities and the more attention you give them the better. Our kids love to chase the chickens around the yard and love when they come up to the house to greet us.

Chickens will come and go

Chickens typically have two good years of laying eggs before egg production decreases, and the feed costs more than you save in eggs. It is up to you, but you can either eat them or keep them as pets and let them die of old age. You can then buy more chicks to start the cycle over again. As mentioned previously, you should be prepared to lose a few chickens along the way. There will always be predators, disease, and natural selection that end up being their demise.

Conclusion

I want to congratulate you for making it to the end of *The Chicken Guide: Incubator to Egg Layer*. Thanks again for taking the time to download and read this book!

You should now have a good understanding of the journey of hatching eggs and raising your chicks to egg layers. While there are many intricate steps to choosing the right hatching eggs, following this easy step-by-step guide will have you raising strong, productive hens that will be laying eggs before you know it!

If you ever have questions or other issues when it comes to the proper raising of chickens, flip open this book. You will more than likely find the answer at your fingertips.

If you enjoyed this book, please take the time to leave me a review on Amazon. I appreciate your honest feedback, which helps me write high-quality books.

Printed in Great Britain
by Amazon

Printed in Great Britain
by Amazon